Praise for *Sawgrass Sky*

"From 'the state with the prettiest name,' as Elizabeth Bishop describes Florida, comes Andrew Hemmert's dazzling debut *Sawgrass Sky*. His poems recount 'a disappearing landscape of sawgrass and smoke,' where the wilderness of panthers and abandoned orange groves contends with the suburbs of Hemmert's youth. Despite development's encroachment, Hemmert establishes himself as a poet of the tropics, rendering lush, otherworldly visions of the natural world. In one gorgeous poem after another, the poet records how velvet night 'slides in like a deadbolt' and starlings flush from sugarcane. He preserves the music of 'reeds rasping against the wind's tongue' and the 'octopus shadows' cast by live oaks. These incantatory poems land like a revelation. Hemmert also dares to observe his world in vulnerable detail. Heir apparent to James Kimbrell's Christ-haunted Florida poems, *Sawgrass Sky* explores an evangelical boyhood in which dads are baptized in backyard swimming pools and sons must become seekers in their own time. Instead of disbelief, Hemmert finds his own paradise, problematic though it is, in the margins of our modern world. This is a young poet's song against forgetting places and people that will not come again, his 'hymn people are forgetting how to sing.' Blessedly, Andrew Hemmert wrote it all down."

—Jennifer Key, author of *The Old Dominion*

"Andrew Hemmert has a scientist's eye and a lyricist's heart. In poems both luscious and austere, he gives life to a version of Florida far removed from the shiny Disneyesque images we've all come to know. His poems are temptingly wild journeys that satiate wanderlust, and readers will not be disappointed in this poet's sensual imagery, deft storytelling, and expansive view of what poetry is. In Hemmert's world, all is nature, and the suburbs hold as much mystery and wonder as the swamps. This book is both incantatory and enchanting. It's a fine debut from a poet who brings us otherworldly beauty in the midst of a compromised world."

—Allison Joseph, author of *The Last Human Heart*

"Andrew Hemmert's *Sawgrass Sky* celebrates the familiarity of the relatable (motifs of home, family, and family history) through the lens of the strangeness and unknowability of elements that surround the quotidian: wilderness, consciousness, and the utterly unknowable. This book's metaphorical depth and lyricism incandesce these narratives that create a unified and beautiful collection."

—William Wright, author of *Blight*

Sawgrass Sky

Sawgrass Sky

Poems

Andrew Hemmert

Texas Review Press
Huntsville, Texas

Printed in the United States of America

Library of Congress Cataloging-in-Publication Data

Names: Hemmert, Andrew, author.
Title: Sawgrass sky : poems / Andrew Hemmert.
Description: Huntsville : Texas Review Press, [2021]
Identifiers: LCCN 2021006448 (print) | LCCN 2021006449 (ebook) | ISBN 9781680032468 (paperback) | ISBN 9781680032475 (ebook)
Subjects: LCSH: Coming of age--Poetry. | Families--Florida--Poetry. | Florida--Poetry. | LCGFT: Poetry.
Classification: LCC PS3608.E4766 S29 2021 (print) | LCC PS3608.E4766 (ebook) | DDC 811/.6--dc23
LC record available at https://lccn.loc.gov/2021006448
LC ebook record available at https://lccn.loc.gov/2021006449

Cover and Interior Design: Bradley Alan Ivey

For my family, and for Lucia

Contents

I

II

III

IV

I

Wildfire

The suburb is tract houses, flattop lawns,
mirror leaf hedges where woodpeckers sleep
on bent twigs and red thread. The suburb rolls out
its roads and sidewalks, its cul-de-sacs
like tent posts staking the world down. The suburb
revolves around safety like the moon,
a chapped gray match head, revolves around
the suburb.

I've had enough silence
on these streets. I'm waiting for one dog to strike
the flint of its voice against the stone-still air,
for that sound to spread through the yards, catching
in a thousand chained and fenced-in mouths.
I wish quiet could always die this way,
one great howl rising up like heat and light.

Father, Son, Ghost

Now the heron-blue fog carries
the world away from itself—
little lake, neighborhood of dogwoods and cul-de-sacs
unraveling to a low, slow breath.

In this light, cigarette light,
ashtray of morning, tell me anything is possible.
Tell me the trees will clap their hands. Tell me this fog
is a voice moving over the surface of the deep,

the one I never learned how to hear.

✦

God of shopping malls. God of disappearing
store signs, of factory clothes
no one will wear. God of bus stops,
God of personal injury lawyers smiling behind blue webs
of graffiti on benches. God of swimming pools—

was your voice in the chlorinated water
that anointed my father's head
when the preacher held him in that suburban pool,
tipped him back like a cup?

I asked my father where it was.
I went there, found a house

abandoned. Weeds needling the concrete driveway,
windows boarded or broken, and the pool drained long ago,

just a green bowl murky with a year of rain.

✦

Every bookshelf, a Bible.
Every morning, a devotion.

I remember the idea of God
was as sturdy in my life

as landscape itself,
or as landscape seems to be

in memory, or a photo album.
And never is, especially

in Florida. Any of us
liable to be swallowed

in our sleep. The idea
of God like the house

that once stood behind
the laundromat, which,

one day in 1981, began
to disappear, one oak sinking

and then the rest of the house
gone, gone with three cars,

a pool. God's voice
like three cars in the earth.

✦

This is a photograph:

my father and I heading out to sea,

the bow of the boat dividing the water

from the water.

✦

The fog rises, slow-winged,
    departs and shows again
the lake with its rushes
    and otters, its carp
periscoping the surface
    of the water, the mallards
in their evergreen arrangements,
    the deep canal where once
I flipped my canoe
    and keeping it from sinking
felt like trying to keep
    the whole lake from slipping under.
Lake of the never-arrived
    voice, the spirit
like so much bread cast out
    and dissolving, dissolving
among the lilies, among
    the ropes and boards
of the spider-strung floating dock.
    Ghost if you were ever here
I never found a way
    to find you, but found
a black snake sleeping
    curled under my canoe,
found old hooks in the mouths
    of bass and pulled them out,
found, despite your absence,
    a way to live,
here where a little wind
    through the cattails is, ultimately,
just that. And lovely still.

Sprawl

Black bears, black bears, lumbering through the suburb
at dawn with their cubs in tow, first animals
molded from mud's shadow, black bears rolling
in the golf course bunker, digging up
the green, snoozing in playground tubes,
black bears dipping their snouts into the ribcage
of the doe that lay dead and broken
in the gutter for days before collapsing
as a wash of flies, black bears spilling
trash cans, ribeye bones and mouth-wet paper
strewn across the lawn, black bears growling
in the slack-jawed rain, their muddy tracks
a map of hunger on my driveway,
black bears rummaging through each garage
left open, knocking over cardboard
boxes of Christmas ornaments that shatter
like hollow eggs, black bears dragging an old man
out of his garden and into the pinewoods
my neighborhood is eating alive, black bear running out
in front of my mother's car, her arm thrown stiff
across my chest, black bear the brakes were screaming
and you didn't look up, you didn't even see us.

Adolescence

august heat thickens a bowl of milk left out the dark slides in like a deadbolt all
night the boy stays up watching roaches crawl across his bedroom floor he keeps a
shoe by his side window the color of a sun-bludgeoned worm only now is the boy
beginning to realize he has a body on his bookshelf sits a weathered leather
bible the gilded pages say he is shameful he hides pictures in his tackle box
his hands are lures his hands insects that never still when one roach climbs up
the bookshelf the boy tiptoes over raises his hollow shoe high the roach opens
its wings and flies away and the boy chases the roach flies into the broken clock on
the wall the boy flies into the broken clock on the wall

Birdhouse

Children of domesticity, of electric light
and cold conditioned air, my brother and I

left our parents' house. Followed the power lines
into the woods behind the suburbs, headed again

to the old tree fort. The power lines hummed like bugs,
it rained all day. The leaves felt like wet newspaper

under our feet. We picked up the biggest sticks
we could find, swung at each other

until they broke—our knuckles raw and palms
full of splinters. All the birds said *I'm here*,

I'm here. We didn't know who built the fort,
how long it had been there in its clearing

under the octopus shadows of the oaks.
It was camouflaged in Spanish moss. The boards

were rotting. Nails the color of old teeth.
Sometimes the fort was a building burning

or a pirate ship. Sometimes we were
pirates and sometimes we were firefighters,

but that day we weren't anything but ourselves
because a birdhouse hung from the fort.

We never saw it before. We never saw anyone else
in those woods. The birdhouse hung from

one of the fort's protruding nails by a bit of unraveling
twine looped through its roof. And rain

falling a little heavier. I got up on my toes
and put my eye to the dark window

of the birdhouse and inside was a wolf spider
the size of my hand. I fell back into the leaves

and they stuck to me like blank nametags.
I brushed them off. I lifted my brother up

so he could see too, and he looked into the birdhouse
like he was looking through a telescope

at some black star—some animal
in our chests looking out onto a world of asphalt

grids and tract houses and not believing
we belonged there, wondering when

we would leave and find anything else.
All eyes and legs and waiting out the rain.

Weather

You need to understand all this, the heft of the canoe
I pulled through the muck of a dried-up canal, coils
of dead lily pads roping my ankles, algae staining
my legs, the lake dropped farther than I'd ever seen, too many
stormless days stranding the bass and bluegill in water so shallow
wakes arrowed off their foreheads no matter where they swam,
the skinny otters dragging the bodies of washed-up gars through
mats of brittle cattails, the few reeds still standing rasping
against the wind's tongue. You need to understand all this
to understand what weather means to me, and why
when hurricane clouds gathered swirling over the lake
I went out barefoot into the rain finally falling, thunder all around
like the walls of the sky settling into themselves again—
why I dared the rain to fall harder, begged it to never let up.

Vessel

We are putting away
    a box of my great grandmother's
glassware, my mother and I,
    trying to determine which pieces
should be placed in which cabinets,
    which are tall enough
to stand unobscured and which need
    to be brought to the forefront,
and it is summer
    like a linen garment left on the lawn
all night that will never dry
    and we must wear it,
I dry the washed water goblets
    and cocktail glasses—
gold-rimmed, the kind of vessels
    originally only brought out
in the right company,
    and now too full of history
to hold anything else—
    with a fraying blue hand towel
as my mother tells me
    about her old high school friends
who are coming over later to visit,
    how we may go into town
for dinner, to walk past
    the bright storefront windows
full of mannequins wearing
    sharp and shining gowns,
and I am thinking of how lovely
    all the women walking the avenue
always seem in their evening
    dresses, a kind of beauty
beyond me, and suddenly

I am sixteen again
and worn out in the heat
and the heart of another summer,
both of my parents gone
for the day, errands or Bible study,
so I go to my mother's closet and take down
a black and slim beach dress
from its hanger, I put it on,
pulling it slow over my head,
leaving the zipper in the back
undone, and I stand there
in front of the full-length mirror,
my belly protruding
through the soft, sequined fabric,
my unimpressive genitalia
looking like something shoplifted
and hidden badly between my thighs,
the thin straps stark
on my pale, skinny shoulders
and I am not like those mannequins,
no breathless machine of plastic and poise,
and I am not like my mother,
no woman, not the body meant
for these dark threads, I am a boy
standing in a dress standing
in his mother's closet
wondering why it doesn't feel strange,
wondering how long
until my parents get home,
and fearing what they might say or do
if they find me here
I struggle back out of the dress
like a bullfrog pulling itself

out of a snake's mouth,
    I bury the dress
at the bottom of the hamper
    and tell no one
for a long time, but now
    I am putting away
my great grandmother's glassware,
    I am handing them to my mother
who places them high up on a shelf
    from which we will probably never
take them down
    to drink from—because they're not meant
for us, just for looking,
    imagining a time, a place,
where such a vessel might fit
    in our hands.

An Orange Grove Full of Bedsheets in November

Brother, soon winter. Soon the frosts that make farmers turn their trees into ghosts

to keep them from dying. There is a way to navigate only by the safety flares

of drowned stars, though neither of us knows how. We only know how winter will

descend like the ending of a news article—colorless, blunt, without epiphany,

just the unbiased grey of leafless maples and the wind-wound bales of Spanish moss.

It's a long time since we've talked. You are still there, shadowed by steeples

in the city that made us. Do you walk to school through cold streets,

through the exhaust of idle cars straining towards heaven like wedding dresses

anchored to lakebeds? Brother, we should say exactly what we mean. We should

believe such a thing was possible. We should trust each other, just for a moment,

while frogs file themselves away in the dirt like letters to no one, and the days

drag on like feuds, the origin of which no one alive remembers.

Frost on the grass like an apology given, taken back.

Boxcars

Moss-stained angels in the cemetery, oaks arcing like smoke
in tired photographs. Roots we can't see, roots we can. Train tracks
past the graves, howl and scrape of distance—

what will deliver us from landscape, from the abandoned splintered lumber
of simply looking out? Row after row of mistakable roads, houses,
a boy in his bed dreaming of lying down between the cold rails,

engines burning through the woods like moonlight. . . In this way
we unhitch our heavy freight. One night, one rusted boxcar at a time.

II

Coyotes

The tracks were already there
when my family moved in,

embedded in the old clay tiles.
They ran through the kitchen, slunk

under the dinner table,
sat still as patience by the front door,

like they were waiting for a letter
to fall through the mail slot.

Sometimes I knelt down, traced the prints
with my finger. I thought desert,

I thought miles and miles of sand
where a little wind could blow away your trail—

and, without history, you could go
anywhere. But even after we moved out

of that house, the coyotes
followed me. They followed me to Ft. Walton.

When my friend's cat went out one night,
scaled the warped wooden fence

and never came back, I knew
what had happened. They followed me

to Illinois—I heard them
in the woods outside the first place

I ever lived alone, their voices
like phosphorescence spreading through

ocean waves I was suddenly so far from.
Their voices jagged as a train horn.

They followed me through tunnels
of highway dark, no one with me

but Joni Mitchell on the stereo
singing their names like cities she can't quit,

and me singing along word for word.
Some mornings I still wake unsure

of what room held my most recent sleep—
as if I could crawl out of bed,

find myself back in that house.
As if I could feel the cool clay

against my feet again, crouch down,
read those tracks like braille: *here I was, here.*

Smokestacks

They shuck the sour black mussels of the coal and swallow them down. They have no hunger, so they borrow ours. Their exhaust plumes hang like a forest of crooked spines, like dented steel wind chimes. Or like seine nets swaying in the waves, shedding scales and grease. They measure the depth of our starless darkness, there is an animal architecture in their steam. And their heaven is full of streetlamp bulbs and plaque-yellow light. They are like angels, unrolling gray scrolls smeared with tobacco paste and gull feathers. Or maybe they are just children building mousetraps in a windowless room.

Rats

in compost piles
and burn piles

in rain gutters
and the rain

in the dirty light
of the sidewalk lamps

night trails them
like their own scarred tails

like lightning
seen in the night

they change the night
they sharpen the dark

when the renovators raised up
their sledgehammers

punched through the plaster
the smell of rot

poured out like water
dead rats stacked

two feet deep in the wall
maggots on their heads

like writhing white crowns
everyone ran out of the house

stood bent over
in the front lawn dry heaving

trying to unbreathe
the rancid air   and only

when the renovators drove away
came back with hazmat suits

could they shovel the bodies out of the wall
like a strange soft coal

when we are alone
we are never alone

they come into our houses
with thirst like a hook

in their jaws   we poison them
the smell rising like a smoke

of black flies   whirring of wings
on our mirrors   black flies of the rats

whirring like saws
on every mirror in the house

have you ever heard an animal
dragging a snap trap

back and forth through an attic
by the bleeding thread

of its limp and useless limb
if you want something

out of your house
it will hurt you

one way   then another

if we ignore them they will split open
the wires in the wall

and from those wounds a fire
red dye crushed

from an untouchable stone
the rats are a canvas

on which I can paint
whatever I feel

they are human because I am
speaking about them

when I lie awake before sleep they are
the thoughts dying and dying

but going nowhere
they are the hands of the sewers

running their claws across the tin
roofs of houses

all that water underneath   rising

I can feel the limestone
eroding beneath me

like the bones of a dog
eaten by rats and soon

giving way   and soon down
into those old caverns

where there will not be silence
there will always be

the slow sound of water on rock
water on limestone

the stalagmites rising up
in their millennial bite

like yellow teeth coming into the mouth
of a night animal

✦

furred and purposeful
tongues of the gothic

they are the broken ghost
of a locked-away child

who steps outside of his little room
and bodiless and bodied

he roams   he sings   he listens

✦

I can't keep invoking them
without invoking myself

I open the snap trap
I poison the food   the sliced apples

the beads of peanut butter
I scoop the half-drowned rat

out of the pool with my net
and fling it across the canal

like nothing but a half-drowned rat
sent soaring   sent somewhere else again

✦

curators of the secret museums
the locked exhibits

full of songbooks
executioners sang to their daughters

after work   I am trying to understand them
beyond disgust   but how can you

praise something you want dead

their voices like a prayer
a firstborn son keeps

underneath his hands   his hands
over his face   fingers intertwined

still that prayer in the mouth   still that prayer
under the surface of the flesh

but I am not going to climb
out of myself   I am not going

to take a hammer to the wall
of my other life   you

will have to sit here with me
as the rats build

their black ladders in our ears

On the Disappearance of the Florida Panther

It is midnight forever in the shadows of their eyes.

Two hundred hungers crouch in the glades, in the reeds,

waiting for a chance to cross the highway. There is blood

and there is gasoline. There is a tract of bottomless grass

into which our fathers' fathers dreamed of falling. So we lived

only on gunpowder. So we brought the dry and the empty

with us. There was a world here. Now we pull up the oil

beneath us like the unstrung hair of the dead. I was the highway.

I carried my walls with me. You might hear a singing

in the trees and it is only a radio. You might

hear a cry in the night and it is only a biologist

trying to prove the numbers wrong. We thought we were the light

as it rises through the branches of the jacaranda,

of the manchineel. We were the fruit that poisons the arrow,

and the fragility of the body. You might hear them

dying in your neighborhood, in your backyard.

Soon we will be more alone than we can even imagine.

Highway Devotional with Abandoned Barns

Now the day drains off like a soft rain falling through the skull
of a farm horse. In the barns by the road, each warped wall
hung with rusty tools is a hymn people are forgetting
how to sing. I've driven a long time, but it feels like I've gone
nowhere. So just outside of Lakeland, I stop on the shoulder,
watch a greyhound chase hundreds of starlings through sugarcane.
The dog lunges again and again until the birds rise away
like the last breath of a bonfire. Then the dog sits back
panting hard, scans the field for something new to follow.
And the barn doors hang open like the wings of dead bats.

Spreading Board

I brought home what I caught,
dropped each insect in the kill jar.
They writhed and twitched
as the acetone-soaked cotton balls
breathed into their bodies. Wasps lasted
the longest. Hours in the jar
and still they clawed at the glass,
trying to climb something they couldn't see.
I could only watch for so long,
slid the jar in the freezer,
nestled it between ice cream cartons
and bags of carrots and peas.
Gradually the spreading board filled up
with rows of figures fragile
as dry reeds. There were katydids,
brassy dragonflies, gray moths
that looked like pieces of bark
broken from the old maple
in my neighbor's backyard. The steel pins
that held them to the board
looked like the keys of wind-up toys or music
boxes, as if three turns to the right
could force a wasp's black wings
to chop the air again, or crank
a song from a cricket's stiff back legs.
It was just an assignment, nothing
made for keeping. And just a few days
into summer, the sharp scent of decay fumed
through my bedroom. I carried
the rotting board out to the curb,
leaned it against the trash can.
Hear me out. If I could take it all back,
find the board half-buried

in the side of some sulfuric hill,
brush off the filth, slide out each steel pin
and watch the insects all come back to life,
rising again into their flight patterns
and their grass-stained music,
I would. I swear.

Three-Legged Deer

When you're always looking for places
  to leave, you place yourself in leaving.

I came home from the bar one night,
  pulled into the apartment parking lot

and a three-legged deer limped
  into my headlights—hobbling,

lurching toward the ground
  with each step. I followed it back

to the ball and chain of the cul-de-sac
  I grew up on, empty canvases

of strange houses, streets I walked
  for no reason but to see where they lead,

the slash pines the deer broke from
  in the velvet hours of night to eat

the flowers of gardens and throw
  their bodies at the mouths of cars.

Sometimes in fog I saw the deer
  close-filed in their processions

on the roadside, almost strung together,
  like dolls cut from construction paper,

so it seemed the softest rain
  could sever their tethers. I've been trying

to hold on to everything that made me,
  disappearing landscape of sawgrass

and smoke, starless cities, the smog-light
  color of the water that gathered

in the mosquito catcher on the front porch
    of a house that was once my home,

sharpening timbre of my mother's voice
    as she called and called for our lab

who had slipped out the unlatched gate,
    out of the backyard's safety and sameness,

disappeared into the neighborhood,
    just following her nose. . . I watched

the maimed deer disappear, awkward,
    slow but determined, into the fog-thin woods

behind the apartments. I sat in the dark
    of the parking lot with my headlights

empty, my car still running.

Corsages

Maybe it's best to let things go.
The past, I mean,

is like an orange grove
abandoned behind broken barbed wire.

Sure, you might find something sweet there,
but mostly it's ants and rats

and possibly a boy
who wants nothing but to sleep

under a collapsing scaffold of blossoms.
A solid, inalienable sleep.

One of the corsages I gave away
was the off-white of a city water tower

in burning August, and the other
was blue, the blue of the sky

on a used car lot billboard.
What became of them, after those dances

where I hardly danced,
is what I'm after now.

What I'm after now, most days,
is permission to dance

like I've made peace with my body.
What I'm after is a lie,

the lie a body can tell a room of people
with no words at all, only footwork,

only hipwork and handwork
and the way shiny shoes in certain light

look like garden shears,
cutting in and out.

Now I only dance drunk,
or alone. And being drunk

is a kind of solitude, just like dancing
can be if you forget the ephemera—

the tuxedos, the buffet stations, the names
of people whose hands and what they did with them

once mattered, somehow, so much.
Bright lights, scuffed leather,

flowers offered in plastic like leftovers.

III

Elegy with Salt at the Root

for George Hemmert, 1931-2006

Somewhere in the smell of the salt, in soot and rot
and the long corridors of blood,
there is a voice, shrinking and shrinking.

If I want to hear it I have to listen hard,
like I'm listening to rain minnows
moving through the gull-haunted tide pools
of spoil islands. Like I'm listening
for ships beneath my feet.

At the end of the Korean War,
my grandfather's cruiser was torpedoed
and went down. And before the ocean
dragged everything under, he saw four of his friends
burn to death in a boiler room.

As long as I knew him, he never talked about it.
He never talked about the smoke
or the screams, where he'd been,
what he'd seen, between the boat's disappearance

and the call out of nowhere
my grandmother received weeks later, doctors telling her
to come collect him from the VA hospital.

He never talked about his mother,
who spent her life in a New York asylum,
watching snow scratch at the windows.

The ocean always comes back, one way or another—
sometimes as voices. Quiet at first,
then louder, persistent, like birds with human mouths
following him from room to room
that no one else could see.

There's a story about a starving man
on a desert island refusing
to eat the gulls within easy reach
of his net, afraid of what they'd swallowed.

There's a story about gulls with bellies
full of lost sailors, bellies full of men.

✦

The first time I heard about the voices—
the cruiser falling out from under my grandfather's feet
like a trapdoor, his friends shriveling in the boiler room—
part of me believed the smoke
from his friends' bodies went into his head.

The doctors turned those voices into lightning.
Turned those voices into convulsions
strapped tight against a table. Turned those voices into pills.

Mostly he was himself—he worked on phone lines,
funneling voices from place to place. He singed
the roof of his mouth on take-out pizza
and drank boilermakers in the kitchen, dropped
the shot glass straight into the mug
so the Old Milwaukee foamed hard,

like troubled water as he drank it all down.
And when, without warning, the pills stopped working—

once, my grandfather claimed to be Jesus.
Once my father stepped off the school bus

and found my grandfather
sprawled out in the street with slit wrists.

✦

My father didn't lie, not exactly,
when he told us we were moving back to Florida
to be closer to family. What my father left out

was my grandfather had called in the night crying,
hearing voices again, and this time the voices
wanted him to hurt my grandmother.

What can you do with a story
like this, something that happened without you
but still has its roots in your blood?

July 2004. Between hurricanes, my father and I
went to help my uncle cut up a live oak
that came down in one of the storms, crashed through the patio screen.

I was twelve. My father and uncle took turns
with the borrowed chainsaw, filled the heavy air
with sawdust. I walked through the yard,
took in the mess. Banana spiders
clung to the mangled screen,
the pool water was a pale chartreuse

from the pollen and leaves that steeped there all night.
For two days we carried that chunked tree

out to the bed of my uncle's truck,
drove it through half-flooded streets
to the mulchers. Powerlines hung limp
like the strings of broken violins,
stop signs leaned crooked where they shifted in the soggy ground.

We left the base of the oak for last.
How strange those roots looked hanging
in the air clumped with mud, the dirt torn away
from the yard where the tree had anchored so long—

anchored, then torn away, and this the space it left.

The ocean always comes back, one way or another.
When my grandfather's kidneys failed, the doctors said
it was the pills—what kept him
from killing himself killed him in the end.

I don't think I understood, seeing him lying there
in the hospital bed, stitched through with tubes,

grown so small under the humming machines.
I didn't understand it in the Catholic church
as the ashes were carried down the aisle like the host,
my father tall beside me in the pew—staring straight ahead,
trying not to cry, his face like brick. I didn't understand it

when one of the sailors in the honor guard
couldn't keep from crying as he stood
stiff-backed in the graveyard,
folded the flag, handed it to my grandmother.

The flag sits in a glass case on my grandmother's mantle—
I think there's still salt in those threads.

What can you do with a story like this? You can fold it up,
put it behind glass. You can float it downstream,
feed it to the birds like bread.
I've tried to forget so much of it

comes down to blood. My blood,
and how patiently those voices can wait.

Voices sink down and fall away,
rise up like water, like tide. Voices
underlying everything—and there is a voice,

so small now it crouches in corners
like a child who is afraid to say anything,

or who has forgotten how. Truth is, I can't recall
the sound of my grandfather's voice.
Only his laughter, which was belly-deep.

Grandfather, give me a few words
to remember you. That's all I'm asking.

Self-Portrait

Fresh scar of dawn. Laughing gulls hovering the shore,
leafing through the Gulf's washed-up burdens—bloated groupers,

moon jellies scattered in the salt-foam sand like the fogged windows of houses
through which almost nothing can be seen.
                                                                  If I could remember

where I'd buried my heart, I wouldn't stand here with my hands in my pockets.
I'd scatter the gulls. I'd start to dig.

Resonate

for Jack McClure

As the noon sun sloughed off the shadows of the cedars, I followed
my grandfather into a field of grass and granite. In my arms,

I cradled a new footstone. We were looking for a man whose blood thrummed
in traces through our arteries, hid under our skin. As we walked

down the rows, scanning for the right name, I read the other markers.
Some carried a hundred years down into the dirt. Some were doll stones,

month-old infants whom sickness claimed before they could learn their names.
When we found the plot, my grandfather gave me his cane, kneeled

on the cement slab. He lifted the eroded marker and set it
in the grass. I put the new stone down in its place. For what

seemed like a long time, we said nothing. Now the old marker
rests on a shelf in my grandfather's garage, under the clutter

of tackle boxes and half-empty bags of potting soil. Maybe
it will still be there when a new family moves into that house,

and maybe a young boy will find it, run his fingers over
the impressions of long-gone letters. Or maybe he'll carry it

into the backyard and lift it over his head, throw it
against a stack of pavers and the fragments will scatter

through what used to be my grandfather's garden like wild gray eggs.
I don't know if my name will outlast me, survive the rain and sun

that scratches us from the world. But that day, there were wasps in the cedars.
They hummed as we walked back to the car, they turned the cedars

into struck tuning forks and that sound, that note, must have traveled down
the trunks, resonating through the roots, ringing the named and nameless bones.

Bright Machines

I built model spacecraft, when I was younger—Saturn rockets,
moon landers, capsules of all eras. I flew them through my bedroom,
my hand the only fuel they needed to soar. And when the television
showed shuttles taking off, their gleaming smoke arcing
over the darkening peninsula, I let myself believe I was part of it.

I wasn't the only kid who saw himself
shining back from the black visor of an astronaut's helmet.
But I felt like I had a better connection than most
because my uncle actually worked with the shuttles.
He was an engineer, oversaw repairs at Kennedy Space Center.
Back then I wouldn't have said it like this,

but I thought my uncle was a bridge between me
and the sky. I saw pictures of the shuttles fastened to the backs of 747s,
heading home from California, and I knew he was there
with them. And that meant I was there too.

When Columbia broke into a burning rain over Louisiana,
fell in pieces into a thousand pastures and backyards,
my uncle joined the search party. It was not a rescue mission. It couldn't be.
The searchers brought the wreckage back to Kennedy,

laid it out in an empty hangar. Separated, catalogued
what was left. And while the debris was still on display,
my uncle took me to see it. We shuffled into the hangar,

two silences in a line of silences. Pathways of black tape
directed our slow procession. On the floor
and on tables, the wreckage lay in labeled piles. Bricks
of heat shield, twisted pieces of metal. Foam insulation—

the same kind of foam that knocked loose on takeoff,
let the atmosphere in as the astronauts tried to make their way
back home. No shredded spacesuits. No broken helmets,

though I knew the search parties found them as they combed through
the scattered landscape. I knew because my uncle told me.
He said he never imagined bringing the shuttle
and the crew home like this—as bags and boxes. As scrap.

If I stared long enough at the individual cordoned-off parts, I got lost
in the infinitesimal. Almost forgot what I was looking at, and the wreckage
started to resemble the same mangle of nails and screws
one might find strewn across a tool shed work bench,
or stuffed in a coffee tin on a hobbyist's desk.
But this wasn't one of my models, and my uncle wasn't a bridge.
And the bright machine, which seven men and women disappeared into,
was lying in charred pieces at our feet.

I put away my models after that. Stopped building them.
I still watched launches, but they were different,
their smoke was serious and distant and I wasn't part of it.
And the shuttles flew, one way or the other.

Jimmy Buffett

I know what people say. He's tacky, bad.
The musical equivalent of lime-a-rita
in a light-up souvenir cup. He brings to mind
American tourists trudging drunk
over foreign shores with the shores of their shoulders
fried with freckles, the smell of a roach

extinguished in an overwatered potted plant.
But when I hear his songs, I think instead
of how my father got home from work
just as my mother was putting my brother and me
to bed. He waited outside the bedroom door

while she prayed, and most nights we could barely keep
our eyes open to tell him how our days went,
already tucked in and tuckered out
in our bunks. But sometimes we were still awake

and asked him for a lullaby. My father didn't know
any lullabies. So he gave us other songs,
songs from his youth—from memories of amphitheaters,
weed smog hovering over rowdy crowds
as Jimmy Buffett half slurred, half shouted
over the din of steel drums and off-key horns—

and so softly my father would begin to sing
"A Pirate Looks at Forty," omitting the verse
in which the speaker admits to having been drunk
for a week and pissing himself in his sleep
in some vague alley in some vague seaside city.

I can see the city. Neon signs all salt-burned,
sticky-floored rum huts, sidewalks strewn with cigarettes,
and all the buildings look like cigarettes
burning from the inside out. My father has his share

of drunken stories, and I do too. At different times,
we both woke up on the floor wrapped in wet towels
and bath mats with our heads feeling like fish bowls

full of boiling. The song isn't a lullaby. It's a dirge.
Sometimes the person I want to be
feels as far away as a locked chest rotting
in the throat of some impossible abyss.
But sometimes I drive through overbuilt beach towns

full of pastel hotels and glaring chain restaurants and Buffett's songs
come on the radio and in spite of everything
they make me smile. I know the words by heart.

Carnival Rides

All the old ones were there,
folded into trailers on the roadside—
Magic Carpet, Pirate Ship, Tornado.
Over the night-smudged scrub woods
the phosphate plants blinked red, and over everything
the stars hung like game targets,
like the ones I always abandoned
after trying, and failing,
to hit them. No luck from the fraying baseballs,
no luck from the chained-down pellet guns.
The Tornado had hard, green seats
that spun your guts right out of you. The only thing
the Tornado carried off
into the distance was itself—
one day spinning in a field, and the next
already headed to another town,
nothing but trash and tire tracks
in the grass to prove a fair had ever been there.
And one night, right as the fair was closing,
I filled my pockets with all the tickets I could find
dropped in the trampled grass
or thrown away among the waste bin's grease-thick
Styrofoam and slick aluminum. Of course
they were worthless. No two carnivals
are the same—even if it's the same field,
the same run-down and rusting
menagerie of rides. But when I drove past the rides
where they slept on the side of that nowhere
two-lane highway, halfway between wherever
they'd left and wherever they were
destined to leave, I remembered a boy
who came home from the fair, for once triumphant.
Who stuffed fistfuls of tickets
in a musty shoebox, slid it all under his bed
like something that would last.

Baptism

where did it go   the water that sanctified me   released me into the sea of my name
the priest cradled my head   lowered me   into the baptismal pool   and then what
the stopper opened   the water given back to pipes   back to sewer and river   back
to duckweed threading current   back to dirty ice   in soda dispensers   back to the
dew that gathers on the grass   like little worlds   of pure light on the green fingers
of the lost   and if it made it back   into the rain   maybe I heard its thunder   the
first time I let my hand linger   on my body   without thinking sin   without
thinking anything but finally feeling   everything as the rain   fell across the roof
like a god made of matchsticks   water in the hands   water in the blood   what was
it anyway   I needed saving from

On Showering

Days gather in the roots
    of my hair—the salt of them,
the sea—and I must send them
    underground, to the rust-
crowded lattice of pipes
    we buried there like instruments
of music unfinished,
    and so I leave my clothes
on the bathroom floor,
    crumpled like bats that fell
asleep midflight, and the water falls
    from the showerhead and I say
thank you to the water
    that touches me and does not judge
the way I survey the bed
    of my body,
does not judge this new
    width around my waist,
or how compulsively
    I search out the skin tags
that have been with me
    so long they might as well be
old ticks turned flesh, and I say
    thank you to the nameless
skin cells sloughing off,
    which are also me, I say
thank you to the lost, long hairs,
    pressing them against
the shower wall like a broken
    word scrawled in a broken cursive,
and I hate to waste anything,
    every night the television

threatens the end, the desiccated
    reservoir of its empty chest,
I know men and women
    could drink this water
I choose to stand in
    longer than I need to,
thinking of everything
    that must be done before sleep
catches me again in its rip
    current, thinking of a woman
I love whom I stood with
    in this same shower
and saw her with my bad eyes
    wash herself, wash her hair
which was curl-thick and cut
    shorter than mine, and as the water
carried off our deadfall
    and our sweat she watched me
in a way I never thought
    anyone would and called me
beautiful, beautiful, I am
    sorry for daydreaming,
I am sorry for feeling
    sorry for myself, I step out
clean, I say thank you
    to the water that washes
what I once was down the drain.

Junkyard at the Florida-Alabama Border

We leave and leave and eventually
we never come back. We leave and we take
our lives with us, we leave our lives behind.

Here the scenery of shacks and pastures
and roadside sweetgums is interrupted,
for a moment, by this collect of rust,

these sagging metal shapes the grass grows through.
I walk between the rows. Junk hunters
press their faces against dust-dulled windows

veined with cracks, fill cloth bags with rear view mirrors.
They rip steering wheels from their stems, stack
hubcaps in cardboard boxes like fine china.

Up the road, the landscape is the same—
only the signs disagree, and the people
who rooted them in cement, anchored them

in this damp, difficult dirt. The same dirt
into which these vehicles will disappear,
years from now. Without fanfare, without

concern for the drivers whose indentations
still cavern the remaining seats. One of the junk hunters
hoists a bumper onto his shoulder,

carries it out to an old red pickup
in the parking lot, and I want to know
how long until that truck comes back to stay.

I want to stay until the junkyard closes,
learn the names of the guard dogs who curl up
comfortable as night under the fenders.

Christmas Eve

for my mother

By now you have unpacked your model buildings,
spread out a white sheet beneath the tree,
rebuilt your winter town. I can see
the post office, the barbershop. The jail

with no one in it. The snowy brownstones,
nothing like any house I remember.
There's a pine made of plastic in each window,
painted with its own flaking ornaments.

I wish I could have made it home this year,
for you more than anyone—you who kept
the peace between us, you who still reach out

through all this distance to remind me
where I come from. I wish I could have helped you
remake your town, one thing that never changed.

Runaway

All things shrink into mirrors. Interstate lights,
crosses zip-tied to fences, distant cities
you notice only as patches of sky glow
where some stars step away from the bodies
we always draw them into. All things shrink
into mirrors—

even the moment

when one radio station is shot through
by another, some symphony succumbing
to the brimstone of a small-town preacher.
It's like the place you're driving away from
trying to keep its hands on you, the invisible strings
threaded through your shoulders finally breaking,
and you not knowing whether the strings
were holding you back or holding you up.

IV

Sawgrass Sky

Florida I've given you too little. Last night you were burning
in the rain—a silver commuter car, the fire reaching from under the hood

and spreading through the paint-sloughing body of the automobile,
that awful salt-gray smoke in the dark like a hot air balloon

made of dust, rising but still staked to the earth. I saw the car
and kept on through the night. You've been burning all year,

sapped by a drought that shriveled lawns to cigarette paper and sharpened
each lighting strike into a wildfire waiting to happen. You've been

burning all year, barely any rain since January, and yet
as soon as my car crossed over the Georgia border your blue skies

fumed with storm clouds. Home again, and you wouldn't be home
without afternoons of thunder crack, the ground shaking like the bolt

was a harpoon taking hold in the dirt and yanking us all heavenward. Florida,
not being here is easier than pitting my parents' God against

my godlessness—the church bell still ringing me awake—or talking to my brother
and reminding myself how little I know about what it means

to be anybody's brother. Down the road there's a place I used to drink
which, after I left home, my brother adopted. It's dark and small, with room

only for a dozen or so patrons, and smells like metal and oysters.
We went there together once, told the bartender we were brothers,

and she squinted at our faces like fine-print maps, said she didn't see it—
whatever she was looking for, whatever landmark would let her believe it.

Sometimes I can't see it myself. And acting like it is another thing entirely.
I remember racing another driver through Lakeland on I-4

while my brother slept in the passenger seat. I pushed my mother's car
to the limit of what caution its speedometer could offer,

the steering wheel shuddering in my hands, and I didn't let off the gas
    until the other driver gave up and fell back, my legs shaking

as I brought the car down to ninety. I could have lost
    my license. I could have killed us both. I want to say it was redemption

when my brother dropped a shot glass in the kitchen years later,
    stepped down hard and drove an overlooked shard deep

into his heel. He limped into my room, shotgunned a beer,
    and I unsheathed the piece from his foot. No redemption, just blood,

just another reason to wash my hands. Florida I'm gone and going
    farther, Illinois already in the rearview mirror

and Michigan on the horizon—lake-effect snow, sidewalks strewn with salt
    and factories abandoned, and in the absence of industry

washed over by the ever-thriving industry of rust.
    There's something about a landscape eating itself that reminds me of you.

In not too many years, the city where I was born will be underwater,
    and the city where my mother was born, and all

her father's family. All our generations drowning in their graves,
    water entering the sand-laced dirt and rolling what's left

of their coffins, rolling them over like anachronistic turbines
    under the grass—as if the only thing after death

was an idiom for regret. Florida I've made you into a graveyard again
    and it's not fair. You're a sawgrass sky, you're swarms of monarchs

like ripe orange groves in migration. You're more than the violence
    we heap on your head like phosphogypsum stacks, more than mugshots

and rubberneckers and the bitter mist that crop dusters drag
    behind them like intangible advertisements. You're more

than one man's regrets. You're more than the house I grew up in,
which isn't mine anymore. I've been turning it over, the moment

when my mother walked in from the backyard
and handed me a garbage bag full of dove nests

she'd swept from the rain gutters. Even then, walking those nests
to the curb, I felt like I was throwing away everything I'd ever known,

all of it bagged and bound for some landfill I might know
only as an acrid note as I passed by on the interstate, or see, rising

like a massive grass-crowned tomb. Down here
our mountains are made of what we no longer need,

or have chosen to abandon. Some birds collect bright threads
and weave them into the dry grass of their nests, so anyone

plucking a loose thread from their shirt could be, without knowing,
donating the weight on their shoulders to the intricate knot

in which two birds perpetuate the idea of flight.
My threads were in those nests. Florida I've flown,

too far and not far enough, on wings of wanderlust and gasoline,
and the reconciliation of any home to the idea of home

is like a car fire in the rain, seen at night, just a glimpse,
so the car might as well be burning still—the rain spitting in the fire's face,

the fire burning regardless, and the occupants
nowhere to be seen. I imagine they ran from the blaze,

knowing the car could explode. Then, even when they arrived
at a safe distance, I think they kept going. Hiked the highway's shoulder,

storm water heavy in their hair, in their clothes,
in the thick night air, turning around every now and again

to see how small they could make the fire just by walking away.

Acknowledgments

My sincere thanks to the editors of the following journals where these poems originally appeared, some in different forms.

The Cincinnati Review: "Smokestacks"

Fantastic Floridas: "Bright Machines" and "Self-Portrait"

Forklift, Ohio: "Jimmy Buffett" and "Vessel"

The Greensboro Review: "Baptism"

Hunger Mountain: "Wildfire"

Iron Horse Literary Review: "An Orange Grove Full of Bedsheets in November" and "Corsages"

Jabberwock Review: "Junkyard at the Florida-Alabama Border"

The Literary Review: "Christmas Eve" (as "Luminaries")

The Louisville Review: "Spreading Board"

Midway Journal: "Adolescence" and "Coyotes"

Mid-American Review: "Elegy with Salt at the Root"

Natural Bridge: "Highway Devotional with Abandoned Barns" and "Rats" (as "A Secret")

North American Review: "On the Disappearance of the Florida Panther"

Poet Lore: "Boxcars" and "Carnival Rides"

Poetry Northwest: "Runaway"

Slipstream: "Weather"

South Dakota Review: "Three-Legged Deer"

Southern Humanities Review: "Sawgrass Sky"

storySouth: "On Showering"

The Swamp: "Father, Son, Ghost"

Tar River Poetry: "Sprawl"

Zone 3: "Resonate"

Thank you to Judy Jordan and Allison Joseph for fostering this manuscript, which started its life as my master's thesis. Jon Tribble was also instrumental in transforming this from a thesis into a book, and I wish I could thank him for it.

Thank you to my Southern Illinois University Carbondale poetry cohort—Kirk Schlueter, Jessica Lynn Suchon, John McCarthy, Lathan Ehlers, Chelsey Harris, and Teresa Dzieglewicz, as well as Anna Leigh Knowles, Meghann Plunkett, Jacqui Zeng, Emily Rose Cole, Alyssha Timm, Seanse Ducken, Joshua Myers, and James Dunlap. You all helped make these poems better, and I can't overstate my gratitude.

Thank you to Meg Flannery Carroll and Maria Romasco Moore, who kept me accountable at our Cristaudo's writing sessions where I composed many of these poems.

Thank you to Katherine Riegel, who got me hooked on poetry as an undergraduate at the University of South Florida, and to Jay Hopler, who invited me into his graduate workshop and encouraged me to keep pushing myself.

Thank you to J. Bruce Fuller for taking a chance on this collection. I'm truly grateful.

Thank you to my parents, my brother Sean, and all the Hemmerts and McClures that comprise my family. This book, my relationship to Florida, wouldn't be the same without your influence on my life, without your stories. I love you all.

Above all, thank you, Lucia, for encouraging me to hold out hope, and for being the most supportive partner anyone could ask for. I love you so much.

About the Author

Andrew Hemmert is a sixth-generation Floridian. His poems have appeared in various magazines, including *The Cincinnati Review*, *The Journal*, *Michigan Quarterly Review*, *Poetry Northwest*, and *Prairie Schooner*. He won the 2018 *River Styx* International Poetry Contest. He earned his MFA from Southern Illinois University Carbondale, and currently serves as a poetry editor for Driftwood Press.